SEE IN 3D

CREATURES OF THE DARK

SEYMOUR SIMON

SCHOLASTIC INC.

New York Toronto London Auckland Sydney
Mexico City New Delhi Hong Kong Buenos Aires

To Wendy Schmalz,
with many thanks for being my agent
and appreciation for being my friend.

ACKNOWLEDGMENTS

Special thanks to Ron Labbe of Studio 3D for his expertise and 3D photo conversions. Thanks also to Alison Kolani for her skillful copyediting. The author is grateful to David Reuther and Ellen Friedman for their editorial and design suggestions, as well as their enthusiasm for this project. Also, many thanks to Gina Shaw, Suzanne Nelson, and Carla Siegel at Scholastic Inc., for their generous help and support.

PHOTO CREDITS

Front cover: © Ronald Austing/Photo Researchers, Inc.; back cover photo and page 22: © Stephen Alvarez/Getty Images; page 1: © Tom McHugh/Photo Researchers, Inc.; page 3: © Arne Hodalic/CORBIS; pages 4, 6, and 24: © Peter & Ann Bosted; page 7: © Bob Krist/CORBIS; pages 8-9: © David W. Kesner; page 10: © B. G. Thomson/Photo Researchers, Inc.; page 12: © Joe McDonald/CORBIS; page 14: © Alan Sirulnikoff/Photo Researchers, Inc.; page 16: © DK Limited/CORBIS; page 18: © Joe McDonald/AnimalsAnimals; page 19: © Dante Fenolio/Photo Researchers, Inc.; page 20: © Charles E. Mohr/Photo Researchers, Inc.

Book design: Ellen Friedman

ISBN 0-439-86649-9

12 11 10 9 8 7 6 5   11/0

Printed in the U.S.A.   40
First printing, October 2006

Can you imagine spending all of your life in complete darkness? That's how it is in a cave. No sunlight, no candles, no lamps, and no electric lights. Yet even in complete darkness, cave animals can find food and can move without bumping into things. They are truly creatures of the dark.

Some of these animals, such as bats, garter snakes, and bighorn sheep, are only part-time cave dwellers. They stay protected in a cave during daylight hours or cold winters. The rest of the time, they live in the outside world. Other animals, such as the cave crab and the cavefish, spend their entire lives in caves. Still other animals live in the semidarkness near cave entrances.

Life in the dark is much different from life in the daylight. In this book, you will see many different creatures of the dark.

Most caves begin as small cracks in the earth. They form when rainwater seeps into soil and picks up a chemical called carbon from rotting plants. The carbon makes the water into a very mild carbonic acid. As this acid water flows downward through the soil, it dissolves underlying limestone rock and begins to form a cave. Over millions of years, small cracks in limestone rock can grow into huge cave systems called caverns.

FUN FACTS

Lechuguilla Cave in New Mexico is 1,594 feet deep. That's deeper underground than the Empire State Building rises above ground.

Some caverns are huge and have rooms bigger than a house. Carlsbad Caverns in New Mexico, Mammoth Cave in Kentucky, and Howe Caverns in New York are some of the biggest. If you put its rooms end to end, Mammoth Cave would stretch for nearly 350 miles.

Many limestone caves have stalactites that hang down from the ceilings. Stalactites look like huge icicles of rock. They form as water drips from the cave ceiling and then evaporates, leaving behind tiny amounts of minerals. Stalagmites grow up from the floor of a cave, usually beneath stalactites. Stalactites have pointy tips while the tops of stalagmites are more rounded.

Some stalactites grow all the way down to the floor, and some stalagmites grow all the way up to the ceiling. Sometimes they meet in the middle to form a column.

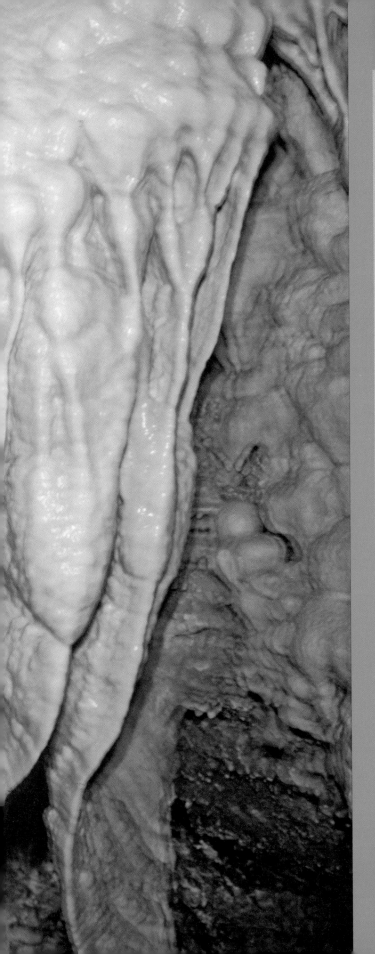

There are many other kinds of cave formations. Flowstone forms when water drips down and covers the walls and floors of a cave. When the water evaporates, sheets of minerals that look like the icing on a cake cover the inside of the cave.

Cave grapes are clusters of small rounded balls or knobs of minerals such as calcium carbonate. Cave pearls form around grains of sand and other particles in cave pools. Gypsum flowers and needles form on the walls and floors of drier caves. Gypsum is a common rock-forming mineral.

Most bats hunt for food outside at night, so they need safe places to sleep during the day. Hanging upside down on cave ceilings, bats are out of reach of most enemies.

Carlsbad Caverns is a daytime home for about one million Mexican free-tailed bats. When night falls, a thick whirlwind of bats spirals out of the cave entrance. Once outside, the bats search for moths, mosquitoes, and other night-flying insects. Using sound echoes, called sonar, each bat can catch and eat hundreds of bugs an hour.

With the coming of dawn, the bats begin flying back to the cave alone or in small groups. They fly high above the entrance, then fold their wings and drop down like stones into the darkness of the cavern. The bats sleep in the cave until they emerge again at twilight.

Other mammals besides bats also use caves for shelter. Bighorn sheep live in the desert mountains and foothills of the American Southwest. For much of the year, the land they live in is dry and almost waterless. During the hot summer, bighorns spend their days in caves to help reduce their water output.

Another cave visitor is the pack rat. It feeds outside at night but returns to the cave at dawn. A pack rat's sensitive whiskers help it to locate food by touch. Its nose helps it to locate food by smell. Pack rats learn to get around in a dark cave swiftly and easily even without sight. If you've ever walked through your room in the dark without bumping into anything, you can see how a pack rat gets used to a route. And in a cave, no one is moving furniture around that might trip up the rat accidentally.

FUN FACTS

Pack rats are also called trade rats. That's because they collect any bright shiny object that they find and leave a nut or a pebble in exchange.

In colder parts of the country, some animals spend the entire winter in caves in a deep sleep called hibernation. During hibernation, the animals look nearly dead. Their heartbeat and breathing slow down. They don't eat or drink. Large masses of crickets, spiders, and even some snakes hibernate in caves.

Snakes, such as these garter snakes, often hibernate in the same cave every year. As the weather warms up in the spring, first the males, and then the females, come out in clusters at a cave entrance. Often there is a writhing mass of newly awakened garter snakes that's bigger than a basketball.

FUN FACTS

Garter snakes are not poisonous, but you might not want to bother them. They give off a really stinky smell if you touch or frighten them.

All animals eat plants, or they eat other animals that eat plants. But most plants need light to grow, so very few plants can grow in dark caves. However, simple plants that need little or no light, such as fungi, algae, and some kinds of moss, grow in caves.

Since there are few plants in caves, the animals that live there depend on food brought from outside. For example, bats visit the outside world to feed and then return to the cave. The droppings that they deposit, called guano, provide food for many other cave animals. Spring floods and streams of water also carry food materials into a cave.

Some cave animals live near the entrance of a cave and trap or hunt other animals that wander in. Cave spiders spin their silky webs just inside a cave and wait for insects, such as flies, moths, cockroaches, and millipedes, to be trapped in the sticky threads.

True cave animals are called troglodytes [TROG-lo-dites], from the Greek words meaning "cave life." They are often eyeless or have poor vision. They are usually pale or white because they have no pigment, or color, in their skin. Outside a cave, their whiteness and poor eyesight would make them an easy target for an enemy. But in the darkness of a cave, they are safe.

Cave crickets, midges, beetles, and other small invertebrates—animals without backbones—can survive in caves, too. They feed on leaves, twigs, and other food materials that are carried into the cave by streams or other animals. Isopods [EYE-so-pods] are small animals with no eyes or skin coloring. They are often found living on cave walls and floors or swimming in cave streams.

If you watch a blind cavefish in an aquarium tank, you can see how easily it swims back and forth without bumping into anything. If living food is placed in the tank, it finds it quickly. In fact, when someone tries to catch one of these fish in a net, it is good at avoiding capture as well.

How do blind cavefish get along so well without eyes? A cavefish has many vibration receptors, called lateral lines, along the sides of its body. These lateral lines help the fish to avoid bumping into rocks or other obstacles and help to locate food. When a cavefish senses a disturbance in the water, such as its prey would make, it swims directly toward it. Water-living cave salamanders also have a sensitive lateral line to assist them in finding food.

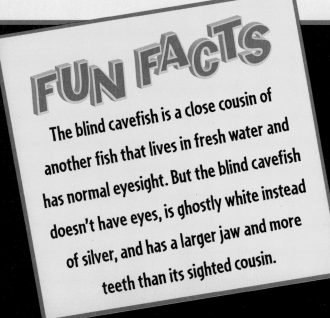

FUN FACTS

The blind cavefish is a close cousin of another fish that lives in fresh water and has normal eyesight. But the blind cavefish doesn't have eyes, is ghostly white instead of silver, and has a larger jaw and more teeth than its sighted cousin.

Animals that live in caves have many special traits that help them to survive. Crayfish or crabs that live outside of caves do a lot of moving in their search for food. If they miss one bit of food, there is always more to be found. Cave animals behave differently. They cannot waste energy in a cave where food is scarce.

A cave crayfish or cave crab moves slowly and stops often. It turns its sensitive feelers from side to side. When one feeler locates food, the other swings around to the same spot. In a short time, the crayfish or crab goes directly to the food and eats it. The cave crayfish wastes very little energy.

Some of the animals that live in caves might be able to live on the outside for a time. But for many creatures of the dark, living in daylight is impossible. By developing special ways of surviving in a cave, they have lost the ability to survive outside. In a sense, a cave animal in sunlight is like a fish out of water.